Contact the authors at www.thatsnoexcuse.org

ISBN: 978-0-578-63934-5

Dedication:

Monica wishes to dedicate this book to Manuel and Sabina, her parents, who taught her the importance of being responsible, accountable, and on-time! And to Jordan, James and Joey, her 3 wonderful sons, who had some unbelievable excuses during their school days!

Jeanine wishes to dedicate this book to her parents, Tom and Joan, who would never let her get away with some of the excuses today. And to her wonderful children, Austin and Taylor, who had their own humorous attendance excuses back in the day!

THAT'S NO EXCUSE

...tales from the high school attendance office

Monica & Jeanine have worked in a high school attendance office for a combined 31 years (M/18, J/13).

Almost everyone in the office, and some of the teachers, have said at one time or another, "You guys should really write a book! You can't make this stuff up!" This book is the result of our years in the attendance office...all the phone calls, forged notes and crazy stories.

Dad comes to attendance window…

"Please don't ask my daughter any questions about her attendance because it stresses her out and causes anxiety!"

Distraught dad comes to the attendance window…

"Well, I need some help from the school…What am I supposed to do?… This country won't let me hit him!"

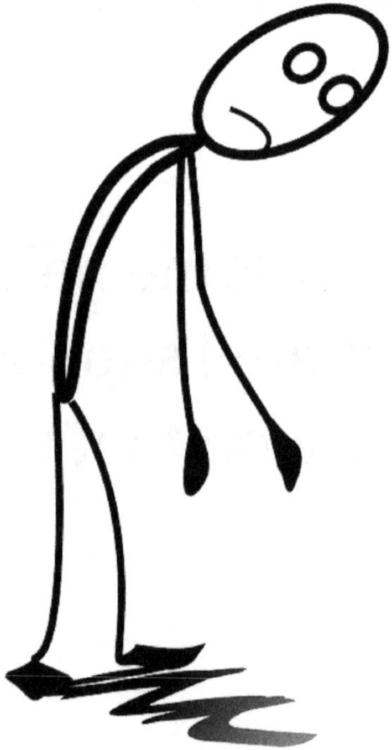

Young girl comes to attendance window…

"My brother has been texting me that he's been falling asleep… so I brought him Starbucks."

Student walks up to the attendance window…

"My stomach hurts."

"Do you want to lie down or go home?"

"No, I really think I need to use the bathroom."

"Okay, why don't you do that and get back to me!"

TEST

First day of final exams…

"Can I speak to the Principal?"

"Why?"

"My doctor told me that I can't take my test or anything…it could be really bad for me if I use my brain too much because I had a concussion."

I sent her to the health office.

Voicemail…

"Please excuse my daughter, Nancy,
for being absent on Friday due to
a sharp pain in her lower back.
She was not able to get out of bed
and had to do some stretch poses
to stand on both feet."

What??
...Are they
witches??

Voicemail…

"They couldn't come to school because it's raining, and they have to walk."

POOPING
Please come
back later

To whom it may concern,
My daughter, Amy, was absent on December 1st because she had a bowel movement the entire day. Please excuse her absence. Thank you.

Mrs. Smith

Student arrives late to school...

"Why are you late??"

"...because I had to help my sick girlfriend!!!"

...he says indignantly.

Voicemail…

"My kids won't be coming to school… because of all the clown stuff!"

HUH???

Voicemail…

"Teenage problems…"
"Doesn't want to come to school!"
"…My son has a really hard time
with zero period."

Note from an ESL student...

I was exostic (sic) from my workout (4:30-9:15pm) that the longest workout of the week. Couldn't make to school on time because after homework. It's almost the midnight already (1:30-2am). So I come. Please give me some more information about homeschool. I can't fix with this kind of school anymore and I can't take it.

Note from parent...

Hello. Good morning, I am asking for a dildo (sic*) because my son was late at school because his foot hurt.

*not sure what they meant, but might be doliendo, which is "hurting" in Spanish??

Student arrives late to school…

"Good morning, why are you late?"

"My sister went into labor and my mom couldn't take me."

Student arrives late to school…

"Why are you late?"

"My aunt just found out she was pregnant and wanted us all there to celebrate!"

While listening to the attendance voicemails, a call was left by a student who identified herself as her mom. She stated that "Trudy" was not in school today because she was home sick.
I called the mom to inform her that her daughter was not in school and that she had forged the phone call. The mom became hysterical and said:

"My daughter would NEVER cut school
or call and pretend to be me!
Call the police!
She must have been kidnapped!"

ZZZZZ

Voicemail…

"My son fell asleep during snack-time and no one woke him up, so he was really late to 4th period! You need to excuse that!"

Note from ESL student…

“…had flu symptoms and a marvelous headache in the morning, but got uh test today. So yeah…go to school!”

A mom came in with her son the day they were going out of town for two weeks for a sports tournament.

"I need to get all of his work."

We explained that there isn't time to get all the work, but her son can email his teachers and much of it is online.

"He's a 14-year-old boy! He's not gonna do that!"

She insisted I give her all of his teacher's email addresses and SHE will get the work for him.

She left saying,

"You're making me feel like a bad mom!"

Voicemail…

"My son is not coming to school due to climate issues!"

There was a girl fight on campus. When one of the student's was brought into the office and asked what the issue was, she exclaimed,

"She was all up in my bubble!"

Student arrives late to school...

"Why are you late on 'late start'...but you had time to go to Starbucks?"

Student holding a coffee, "Actually, it's their fault...they were taking too long"

Frantic phone call from a mom…

"I need you to release my son right now! He has to come home because our dog is sick, and he needs to help me put our dog in the car…he is really big, and I can't do it by myself!"

A legal complaint was filed against a mom because of her son's truancy. She was told she may be fined $$$ if her son was not in school and on-time every day. She called the office about 5 minutes before school...

"I'm at the stop light one block from the school and Albert just jumped out of the car and is running toward Big Lots! Please tell the principal that I did my part... I tried to get him to school on-time...this is not my fault!"

We received a phone call from a doctor's office...a parent was in their office asking for a doctor's note to excuse her daughter from 2 weeks of school so they could leave early for a winter vacation break...

The mom told the doctor's office, *"the school won't excuse her absences unless we have a doctor's note."*

(parent didn't quite understand!)

Voicemail…

"My son did not attend first period because he spilled his protein shake all over his clothes at zero period, therefore he went to the office to wait for me to bring him a change of clothes. Please excuse his absence from first period."

Note from ESL student...

I accidentally food poisoned myself on Saturday because no one at home so I had to cook. Ended up messing up my already messed up epigenetic clock. I couldn't sleep until morning 8am to a constant headache. It was really bad...sorry for being late to school, no choice.

A student brought a kitten to school in his backpack! He handed it to a female student who was caught by the teacher with the kitten. When she was interviewed by the Assistant Principal, she stated,
"This is my emotional support cat."
The principal called the girl's mom, who said,
"What cat? We don't have a cat?!"

When the girl texted the boy who originally had the kitten, he came up to the office, grabbed the kitten and they both ran off campus.

Numerous voicemails throughout the year from one parent regarding their student…

"My student is being pushed too hard by the institution to attend first period. She is not in school today due to psychological reasons."

"…not in school…probably psychological due to the late start schedule."

"…absent due to psychological reasons because her on-line boyfriend broke up with her at midnight."

"…not in school due to psychological issue brought on by the truancy letter sent home by the district office."

"…psychological issues due to the devastation of being sent to the DA's office for excessive absences and truancy."

I received a call from a parent asking why she got a call regarding her daughter's absence…

"She was on the field trip to the amusement park with ASB!"

"What field trip? There wasn't a field trip?"

"Yes, there was! I signed the permission slip!"

I checked with ASB and there wasn't a field trip. The student had forged the field trip notice and had their parent sign.

(You gotta give this "straight A" student credit for being imaginative!)

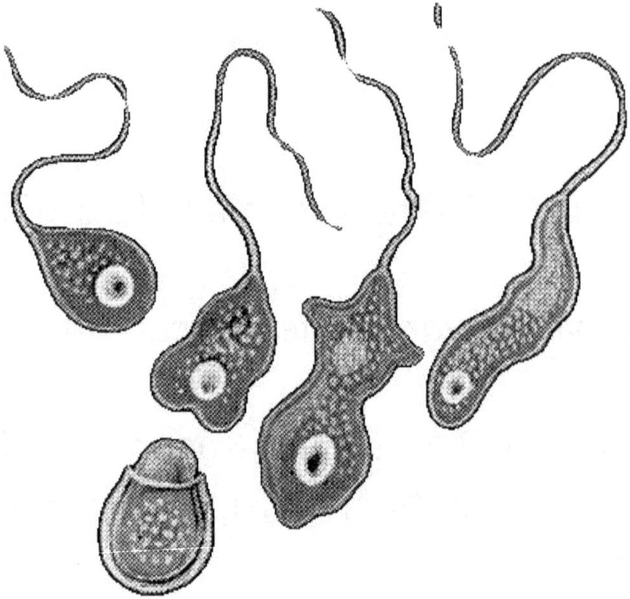

A 15-year old student had excessive absences to school. Mom kept insisting he had a medical condition. We asked for doctor's notes for any absences due to illness. We received multiple Dr. notes stating the student was a patient at a sperm bank. We followed up, found out mom worked at the sperm bank and had forged numerous notes on her son's behalf.

(She doesn't work there anymore!

Voicemail…

"My son's backpack broke, so he couldn't go to 2nd or 4th period."

(huh…what about the other classes?)

MOM

I called a mom regarding excessive absences...

She said, "I'm a single mom with 6 kids, so that's why he is late sometimes!"
I asked if she had received his report card (6 F's)...
She said, "Yes."
...I was at a loss for words!

I received a phone call from a woman demanding I clear all her daughter's absences so she could make up the schoolwork she missed...
I told her, "I just spoke to Amy's father yesterday and he said his wife only speaks Spanish!" She hung up on me.
I found out later that the woman was Amy's boyfriend's mom!

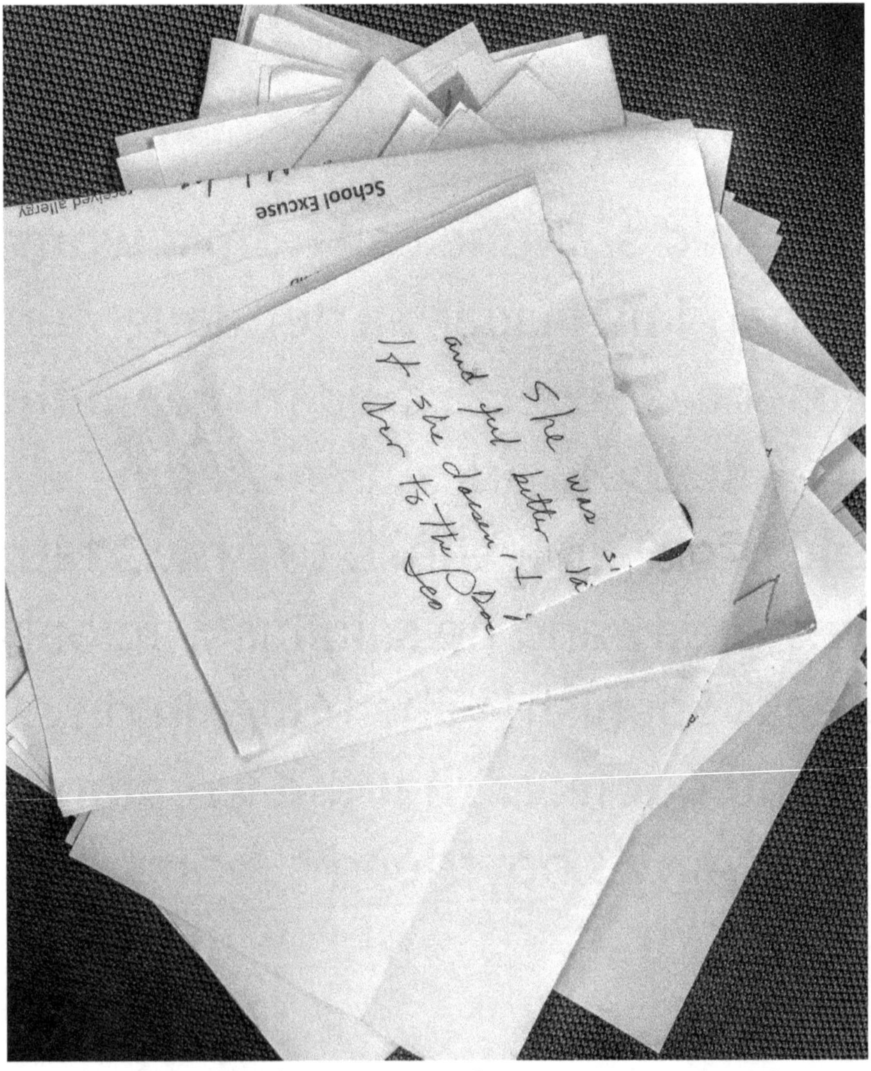

....and they just keep coming!

CPSIA information can be obtained
at www.ICGtesting.com
Printed in the USA
LVHW101008240420
654380LV00009B/1314

9 780578 639345